Stella
He Sees You!

2-3-19

MY
DAILY GRATITUDE
JOURNAL

Printed in the United States of America

First Printing, 2018

ISBN-13:
978-1729562277

ISBN-10:
1729562272

Cover & Interior Design by:
McKenzie Matlock

www.dukematlock.com

City of Refuge
CHILDREN'S HOME GT

A portion of all journal sales will be donated to City of Refuge Children's Home GT.

To learn more about City of Refuge, visit http://www.corgt.com

THIS JOURNAL BELONGS TO:

_____

TABLE OF CONTENTS

ACKNOWLEDGEMENTS

A few years ago, I was going through an incredibly difficult time in my life. It was apparent to my family. For Christmas that year, my daughter gave me a jar she had decorated filled with handwritten notes of encouragement, scriptures, and quotes. She said, "Whenever you're feeling down, pull one of these notes out and read it. Hopefully they will make you feel a little better." I followed her instructions and her notes did just that, I felt better! They changed my thought pattern from negative to positive. It's evident to me that my thoughts matter.

Creating a daily gratitude journal was an idea that first sprouted out of the relationships I have with my coaching clients. I firmly believe that our thoughts have the ability to bring life or death to every area of our lives. Our thoughts shape what we believe. Daily gratitude is a part of the Get Up and Grow process, as laid out in my book *Get Up & Grow: 21 Habits of Successful People*. Through my coaching relationships I realized the importance of showing gratitude and the impact it can have on our thoughts and lives. My team and I came to the conclusion that it was important to create a journal solely dedicated to showing gratitude.

Now, on to why we are here, for me to acknowledge those who helped make this journal happen and show my gratitude! First, thank you McKenzie for that jar! It was a game changer. Thank you Kelley for the kind words and encouragement you offer each day. You have allowed me the freedom to pursue every dream. You're a wonderful wife. I'd like to thank the Invest Leadership team, Andrea, Dawn, Megan, and McKenzie. Thank you all for the research you put in to bringing this journal together. I couldn't have done it without you. McKenzie, thank you for the interior layout and cover design. I would also like to thank each of my coaching clients. Thank you for allowing me to be a part of your lives and your success journeys. I have learned more from you than you could ever know. I would also like to thank God for rescuing me and filling my life with hope.

INTRODUCTION

Gratitude is an attitude that has to be cultivated all year round. Self-deprecating thoughts are like weeds; they are useless, yet possess the ability to take over completely. Negativity is one of the most common agents of destruction when dealing with growth, success, and progress. Sometimes we are pessimistic about our circumstances; maybe we feel stuck or trapped. Other times we are negative about ourselves; defeatist self-talk can make us believe that we will never be good enough to accomplish our goals.

So what can we do when negative thoughts are taking root in our minds? The best way to overcome negativity is by cultivating an attitude of gratitude. Fill your mind with things you are grateful for and you'll find there's no room left for worry or self-doubt.

And that's where this journal comes in. It's called My Daily Gratitude Journal. Start or end your day on a positive note with statements of gratitude — the more you practice it, the easier it will become!

If you can't think of what to be grateful for, here is a list to help you get started each day:

1. Be grateful for the encouragers in your life.
2. Be grateful for the journey you are on.
3. Be grateful for family and friends.
4. Be grateful for small victories.

Gratitude is hard sometimes, especially when you feel discouraged; but there is nothing that shifts perspectives quite like being thankful. Be specific when you write down your daily gratitude. See how your everyday life transforms when you make thankfulness a priority!

"Gratitude and attitude are not challenges; they are choices.

-Robert Braathe

Daily Gratitude:

Date: __ / __ / __

_____
_____
_____
_____
_____
_____
_____
_____
_____

"Gratitude unlocks the fullness of life. It turns what we have into enough, and more."

- Melody Beattie -

Daily Gratitude:

Date: __ / __ / __

_____
_____
_____
_____
_____
_____
_____
_____
_____

"I would maintain that thanks are the highest form of thought; and that gratitude is happiness doubled by wonder."

- G.K. Chesterson -

Daily Gratitude: Date: __ /__ /__

_____
_____
_____
_____
_____
_____
_____
_____

"Rejoice always, pray continually, give thanks in all circumstances; for this is God's will for you in Christ Jesus."

- 1 Thessalonians 5:16-18 -

Daily Gratitude: Date: __ /__ /__

_____
_____
_____
_____
_____
_____
_____
_____

"As we express our gratitude, we must never forget that the highest appreciation is not to utter words, but to live by them."

- John F. Kennedy -

Daily Gratitude: Date: __ / __ / __

_____

_____

_____

_____

_____

_____

_____

_____

_____

"Gratitude is riches. Complaint is poverty."

- Doris Day -

Daily Gratitude: Date: __ / __ / __

_____

_____

_____

_____

_____

_____

_____

_____

*"Develop an attitude of gratitude, and give thanks for everything
that happens to you, knowing that every step forward is a step
toward achieving something bigger and better than your current
situation."*

- Brian Tracy -

Daily Gratitude:

_____
_____
_____
_____
_____
_____
_____
_____
_____

"I will give thanks to the Lord because of his righteousness; I will sing the praises of the name of the Lord Most High."

- Psalm 7:17 -

Daily Gratitude:

Date: __ / __ / __

_____
_____
_____
_____
_____
_____
_____
_____

"Reflect upon your present blessings, of which every man has plenty; not on your past misfortunes, of which all men have some."

- Charles Dickens -

Daily Gratitude: Date: __ / __ / __

_____

_____

_____

_____

_____

_____

_____

_____

_____

"Acknowledging the good that you already have in your life is the foundation for all abundance."

- Eckhart Tolle -

Daily Gratitude: Date: __ / __ / __

_____

_____

_____

_____

_____

_____

_____

_____

"Gratitude is a currency that we can mint for ourselves, and spend without fear of bankruptcy."

- Fred De Witt Van Amburgh -

Daily Gratitude:

Date: __ /__ /__

_____
_____
_____
_____
_____
_____
_____
_____

"I will extol the Lord at all times; his praise will always be on my lips."

- Psalm 34:1 -

Daily Gratitude:

Date: __ /__ /__

_____
_____
_____
_____
_____
_____
_____
_____

"Things turn out best for people who make the best of the way things turn out."

- John Wooden -

Daily Gratitude:

Date: __ / __ / __

_____
_____
_____
_____
_____
_____
_____
_____
_____

"This is a wonderful day. I've never seen this one before."

- Maya Angelou -

Daily Gratitude:

Date: __ / __ / __

_____
_____
_____
_____
_____
_____
_____
_____

"Rest and be thankful."

- William Wordsworth -

Daily Gratitude: Date: __ / __ / __

_____

_____

_____

_____

_____

_____

_____

_____

"Gratitude can transform common days into thanksgivings, turn routine jobs into joy, and change ordinary opportunities into blessings."

- William Arthur Ward -

Daily Gratitude: Date: __ / __ / __

_____

_____

_____

_____

_____

_____

_____

_____

"I dwell in possibility."

- Emily Dickinson -

Daily Gratitude:

_____
_____
_____
_____
_____
_____
_____
_____

"Give praise to the Lord, proclaim his name; make known among the nations what he has done."

- 1 Chronicles 16:8 -

Daily Gratitude:

Date: _ /_ /_

_____
_____
_____
_____
_____
_____
_____
_____

"It is our attitude at the beginning of a difficult task which, more than anything else, will affect its successful outcome."

- William James -

Daily Gratitude:

_____

_____

_____

_____

_____

_____

_____

_____

_____

"I don't have to chase extraordinary moments to find happiness – it's right in from of me if I'm paying attention and practicing gratitude."

- Brene Brown -

Daily Gratitude:

Date: __ /__ /__

_____

_____

_____

_____

_____

_____

_____

_____

_____

"Those blessings are the sweetest that are won with prayer and worn with thanks."

- Thomas Goodwin -

"Give thanks to the Lord, for he is good; his love endures forever.

-Psalm 106:1

Daily Gratitude: Date: __ / __ / __

_____

_____

_____

_____

_____

_____

_____

_____

"Fill the Earth with your songs of gratitude."

- Charles Spurgeon -

Daily Gratitude: Date: __ / __ / __

_____

_____

_____

_____

_____

_____

_____

_____

"The way to know life is to love many things."

- Vincent Van Gogh -

Daily Gratitude:

_____
_____
_____
_____
_____
_____
_____
_____
_____

"Enjoy the little things, for one day you may look back and realize they were the big things."

- Robert Brault -

Daily Gratitude:

Date: __ / __ / __

_____
_____
_____
_____
_____
_____
_____
_____
_____

"How very little can be done under the spirit of fear."

- Florence Nightingale -

Daily Gratitude:

Date: __ /__ /__

_____
_____
_____
_____
_____
_____
_____
_____
_____

"No one who achieves success does so without acknowledging the help of others. The wise and confident acknowledge this help with gratitude."

- Alfred North Whitehead -

Daily Gratitude:

Date: __ /__ /__

_____
_____
_____
_____
_____
_____
_____
_____

"Remember when life's path is steep to keep your mind even."

- Horace -

Daily Gratitude: Date: __ /__ /__

_____
_____
_____
_____
_____
_____
_____
_____
_____

"Do not be anxious about anything, but in every situation, by prayer and petition, with thanksgiving, present your requests to God."

- Philippians 4:6 -

Daily Gratitude: Date: __ /__ /__

_____
_____
_____
_____
_____
_____
_____
_____
_____

"A contented mind is the greatest blessing a man can enjoy in this world."

- Joseph Addison -

Daily Gratitude:

_____
_____
_____
_____
_____
_____
_____
_____

"Believe you can and you're halfway there."

- Theodore Roosevelt -

Daily Gratitude:

Date: __ / __ / __

_____
_____
_____
_____
_____
_____
_____
_____

"Positive anything is better than negative nothing."

- Elbert Hubbard -

Daily Gratitude: Date: __ /__ /__

_____

_____

_____

_____

_____

_____

_____

_____

_____

"Appreciation is a wonderful thing: It makes what is excellent in others belong to us as well."

- Voltaire -

Daily Gratitude: Date: __ /__ /__

_____

_____

_____

_____

_____

_____

_____

_____

_____

"The thankful receiver bears a plentiful harvest."

- William Blake -

Daily Gratitude: Date: __ /__ /__

_____
_____
_____
_____
_____
_____
_____
_____

"The Lord has done it this very day; let us rejoice and be glad."

- Psalm 118:24 -

Daily Gratitude: Date: __ /__ /__

_____
_____
_____
_____
_____
_____
_____
_____

"The unthankful heart discovers no mercies; but the thankful heart will find, in every hour, some heavenly blessings."

- Henry Ward Beecher -

Daily Gratitude: Date: __ /__ /__

_____
_____
_____
_____
_____
_____
_____
_____
_____

"Silent gratitude isn't very much use to anyone."

- Gertrude Stein -

Daily Gratitude: Date: __ /__ /__

_____
_____
_____
_____
_____
_____
_____
_____
_____

"We can complain because rose bushes have thorns, or rejoice because thorns have roses."

- Alphonse Karr -

Daily Gratitude: Date: _ / _ / _

_____

_____

_____

_____

_____

_____

_____

_____

"Keep your face to the sunshine and you cannot see a shadow."

- Helen Keller -

Daily Gratitude: Date: _ / _ / _

_____

_____

_____

_____

_____

_____

_____

_____

"We should certainly count our blessings, but we should also make our blessings count."

- Neal A. Maxwell -

"We would worry less if we praised more. Thanksgiving is the enemy of discontent and dissatisfaction.

-H.A. Ironside

Daily Gratitude: Date: __ /__ /__

_____
_____
_____
_____
_____
_____
_____
_____

"Let the peace of Christ rule in your hearts, since as members of one body you were called to peace. And be thankful."

- Colossians 3:15 -

Daily Gratitude: Date: __ /__ /__

_____
_____
_____
_____
_____
_____
_____
_____

"Appreciation can make a day, even change a life. Your willingness to put it into words is all that is necessary."

- Margaret Cousins -

Daily Gratitude:

_____

_____

_____

_____

_____

_____

_____

_____

"The art of being happy lies in the power of extracting happiness from common things."

- Henry Ward Beecher -

Daily Gratitude:

Date: __ /__ /__

_____

_____

_____

_____

_____

_____

_____

_____

"Joy is a heart full and a mind purified by gratitude."

- Marietta McCarty -

Daily Gratitude: Date: __ /__ /__

_____

_____

_____

_____

_____

_____

_____

_____

"A pessimist sees the difficulty in every opportunity, an optimist sees the opportunity in every difficulty."

- Winston Churchill -

Daily Gratitude: Date: __ /__ /__

_____

_____

_____

_____

_____

_____

_____

_____

"Choosing to be positive and having a grateful attitude is going to determine how you're going to live your life."

- Joel Osteen -

Daily Gratitude: Date: __ /__ /__

_____

_____

_____

_____

_____

_____

_____

_____

_____

"Consider it pure joy, my brothers and sisters, whenever your face trials of many kinds, because you know that the testing of your faith produces perseverance."

- James 1:2-3 -

Daily Gratitude: Date: __ /__ /__

_____

_____

_____

_____

_____

_____

_____

_____

"A positive attitude causes a chain reaction of positive thoughts, events, and outcomes. It is a catalyst and it sparks extraordinary results."

- Wade Boggs -

Daily Gratitude:

_____
_____
_____
_____
_____
_____
_____
_____

"Let gratitude be the pillow upon which you kneel to say your nightly prayer. And let faith the bridge you build to overcome evil and welcome good".

- Maya Angelou -

Daily Gratitude:

Date: _ /_ /_

_____
_____
_____
_____
_____
_____
_____
_____

"Keep your eyes open to your mercies. The man who forgets to be thankful has fallen asleep in life."

- Robert Louis Stevenson -

Daily Gratitude: Date: _ /_ /_

_____
_____
_____
_____
_____
_____
_____
_____
_____

"Happiness cannot be traveled to, owned, earned, worn or consumed. Happiness is the spiritual experience of living every minute with love, grace, and gratitude."

- Denis Waitley -

Daily Gratitude: Date: _ /_ /_

_____
_____
_____
_____
_____
_____
_____
_____
_____

"Gratitude is the sign of noble souls."

- Aesop Fables -

Daily Gratitude: Date: __ /__ /__

_____
_____
_____
_____
_____
_____
_____
_____
_____

"This is the day that the Lord has made; let us rejoice and be glad in it."

- Psalm 118:24-

Daily Gratitude: Date: __ /__ /__

_____
_____
_____
_____
_____
_____
_____
_____
_____

"There's no happier person than a truly thankful, content person."

- Joyce Meyer -

Daily Gratitude:

Date: __ / __ / __

_____

_____

_____

_____

_____

_____

_____

_____

_____

"Be grateful for what you have and stop complaining – it bores everybody else, does you no good, and doesn't solve any problems."

- Zig Ziglar -

Daily Gratitude:

Date: __ / __ / __

_____

_____

_____

_____

_____

_____

_____

_____

"If a fellow isn't thankful for what he's got, he isn't likely to be thankful for what he's going to get."

- Frank A. Clark -

Daily Gratitude: Date: _ /_ /_

_____
_____
_____
_____
_____
_____
_____
_____

"Be thankful for what you have; you'll end up having more. If you concentrate on what you don't have, you will never, ever have enough."

- Oprah Winfrey-

Daily Gratitude: Date: _ /_ /_

_____
_____
_____
_____
_____
_____
_____
_____

"The best way to show my gratitude to God is to accept everything, even my problems, with joy."

- Mother Teresa -

Daily Gratitude: Date: __ / __ / __

_____

_____

_____

_____

_____

_____

_____

_____

_____

"Therefore let us be grateful for receiving a kingdom that cannot be shaken, and thus let us offer to God acceptable worship, with reverence and awe."

- Hebrews 12:28 -

Daily Gratitude: Date: __ / __ / __

_____

_____

_____

_____

_____

_____

_____

_____

_____

"God gave you a gift of 84,600 seconds today. Have you used one of them to say thank you?"

- William Arthur Ward -

Daily Gratitude:

_____
_____
_____
_____
_____
_____
_____
_____
_____

"Appreciation and gratitude are a must if you choose to become the architect of increased happiness and your own fulfillment."

- Doc Childre -

Daily Gratitude:

Date: __ /__ /__

_____
_____
_____
_____
_____
_____
_____
_____

"The person who send out positive thoughts activates the world around him positively and draws back to himself positive results."

- Norman Vincent Peale -

"I will give thanks to you, Lord, with all my heart. I will tell of all your wonderful deeds.

-Psalm 9:1

Daily Gratitude:

_____
_____
_____
_____
_____
_____
_____
_____
_____

"If you count all your assets, you always show a profit."

- Robert Quillen -

Daily Gratitude:

Date: __ /__ /__

_____
_____
_____
_____
_____
_____
_____
_____
_____

"Be sure to put your feet in the right place, then stand firm."

- Abraham Lincoln -

Daily Gratitude:

Date: __ / __ / __

_____
_____
_____
_____
_____
_____
_____
_____
_____

"Wherever you go, no matter what the weather, always bring your own sunshine."

- Anthony J. D'Angelo -

Daily Gratitude:

Date: __ / __ / __

_____
_____
_____
_____
_____
_____
_____
_____

"Yesterday is not ours to recover, but tomorrow is ours to win or lose."

- Lyndon B. Johnson -

Daily Gratitude:

Date: __ /__ /__

_____

_____

_____

_____

_____

_____

_____

_____

"But thanks be to God! He gives us the victory through our Lord Jesus Christ."

- 1 Corinthians 15:57 -

Daily Gratitude:

Date: __ /__ /__

_____

_____

_____

_____

_____

_____

_____

_____

"The more I give thanks, the more reasons I have for gratitude."

- Michael Hyatt -

Daily Gratitude: Date: __ / __ / __

_____

_____

_____

_____

_____

_____

_____

_____

"The unthankful heart discovers no mercies; but the thankful heart will find, in every hour, some heavenly blessings."

- Henry Ward Beecher -

Daily Gratitude: Date: __ / __ / __

_____

_____

_____

_____

_____

_____

_____

_____

"The hardest arithmetic to master is that which enables us to count our blessings."

- Eric Hoffer -

Daily Gratitude: Date: __ /__ /__

_____

_____

_____

_____

_____

_____

_____

_____

"Where God guides, He provides. No matter how things look, God is still in control. Stay in peace and be hopeful. Your blessing is coming soon."

- Germany Kent -

Daily Gratitude: Date: __ /__ /__

_____

_____

_____

_____

_____

_____

_____

_____

"Don't just count your blessings; Be the blessing other people count on."

- Mark Amend -

Daily Gratitude: Date: __ / __ / __

_____
_____
_____
_____
_____
_____
_____
_____
_____

"I thank Christ Jesus our Lord, who has given me strength, that he considered me faithful, appointing me to his service."

- 1 Timothy 1:12 -

Daily Gratitude: Date: __ / __ / __

_____
_____
_____
_____
_____
_____
_____
_____

"I try to live what I teach. A lot of things come against us in life, but we should try to find something to be grateful for, and see each day as a gift."

- Joel Osteen -

Daily Gratitude:

Date: __ /__ /__

_____
_____
_____
_____
_____
_____
_____
_____

"I am not what happened to me. I am what I choose to become."

- Carl Jung -

Daily Gratitude:

Date: __ /__ /__

_____
_____
_____
_____
_____
_____
_____
_____

"Feeling gratitude and not expressing it is like wrapping a present and not giving it."

- William Arthur Ward -

Daily Gratitude:

Date: __ / __ / __

_____
_____
_____
_____
_____
_____
_____
_____
_____

"If you want to turn your life around, try thankfulness. It will change your life mightily."

- Gerald Good -

Daily Gratitude:

Date: __ / __ / __

_____
_____
_____
_____
_____
_____
_____
_____

"And whatever you do, whether in word or deed, do it all in the name of the Lord Jesus, giving thanks to God the Father through him."

- Colossians 3:17 -

Daily Gratitude: Date: __ /__ /__

_____

_____

_____

_____

_____

_____

_____

_____

"Embrace your life journey with gratitude, so that how you travel your path is more important than reaching your ultimate destination."

- Rosalene Glickman -

Daily Gratitude: Date: __ /__ /__

_____

_____

_____

_____

_____

_____

_____

_____

"Enjoy the little things, for one day you may look back and realize they were the big things."

- Robert Brault -

Daily Gratitude: Date: __ / __ / __

_____
_____
_____
_____
_____
_____
_____
_____

"You pray in your distress and in your need; would that you might also pray in the fulness of your joy and in your days of abundance."

- Khalil Gibran -

Daily Gratitude: Date: __ / __ / __

_____
_____
_____
_____
_____
_____
_____
_____

"The way to develop the best that is in a person is by appreciation and encouragement."

- Charles Schwab -

Daily Gratitude: Date: __ /__ /__

_____

_____

_____

_____

_____

_____

_____

_____

"I will praise God's name in song and glorify him with thanksgiving."

- Psalm 69:30 -

Daily Gratitude: Date: __ /__ /__

_____

_____

_____

_____

_____

_____

_____

_____

"While you are going through your trial, you can recall your past victories and count the blessing that you do have with a sure hope of greater ones to follow if you are faithful."

- Ezra Taft Benson -

" When it comes
to life the
critical thing is
whether you
take things for
granted or take
them with
gratitude.

-G.K. Chesterson

Daily Gratitude:

Date: __ /__ /__

_____
_____
_____
_____
_____
_____
_____
_____

"Gratitude is the memory of the heart."

- Jean Baptiste Massieu -

Daily Gratitude:

Date: __ /__ /__

_____
_____
_____
_____
_____
_____
_____
_____

"If you have lived, take thankfully the past."

- John Dryden -

Daily Gratitude: Date: __ /__ /__

_____
_____
_____
_____
_____
_____
_____
_____

"As each day comes to us refreshed and anew, so does my gratitude renew itself daily."

- Terri Guillemets -

Daily Gratitude: Date: __ /__ /__

_____
_____
_____
_____
_____
_____
_____
_____

"Give thanks to the God of heaven. His love endures forever."

- Psalm 136.26 -

Daily Gratitude: Date: __ /__ /__

_____

_____

_____

_____

_____

_____

_____

_____

*"We can only be said to be alive in those moments when our
hearts are conscious of our treasures."*

- Thornton Wilder -

Daily Gratitude: Date: __ /__ /__

_____

_____

_____

_____

_____

_____

_____

_____

*"Gratitude is a quality similar to electricity: it must be produced
and discharged and used up in order to exist at all."*

- William Faulkner -

Daily Gratitude:

Date: __ /__ /__

_____
_____
_____
_____
_____
_____
_____
_____
_____

"Ingratitude is the daughter of pride."

- Miguel De Cervantes -

Daily Gratitude:

Date: __ /__ /__

_____
_____
_____
_____
_____
_____
_____
_____

"When our perils are past, shall our gratitude sleep?"

- George Canning -

Daily Gratitude:

_____
_____
_____
_____
_____
_____
_____
_____

"Devote yourselves to prayer, being watchful and thankful."

- Colossians 4:2 -

Daily Gratitude:

Date: __ /__ /__

_____
_____
_____
_____
_____
_____
_____
_____

"Gratitude is an opener of locked-up blessings."

- Marianne Williamson -

Daily Gratitude: Date: __ / __ / __

_____

_____

_____

_____

_____

_____

_____

_____

_____

"Hem your blessings with thankfulness so they don't unravel."

- Author Unknown -

Daily Gratitude: Date: __ / __ / __

_____

_____

_____

_____

_____

_____

_____

_____

"Kindness in words creates confidence. Kindness in thinking creates profoundness. Kindness in giving creates love."

- Lao Tzu -

Daily Gratitude: Date: __ /__ /__

_____
_____
_____
_____
_____
_____
_____
_____

"No duty is more urgent than that of returning thanks."

- James Allen -

Daily Gratitude: Date: __ /__ /__

_____
_____
_____
_____
_____
_____
_____
_____

"Gratitude is something of which none of us can give too much."

- A.J. Cronin -

Daily Gratitude: Date: __ / __ / __

_____
_____
_____
_____
_____
_____
_____
_____

"Thanks be to God for his indescribable gift!"

- 2 Corinthians 9:15 -

Daily Gratitude: Date: __ / __ / __

_____
_____
_____
_____
_____
_____
_____
_____

"The smallest act of kindness is worth more than the grandest intention."

- Oscar Wilde -

Daily Gratitude: Date: __ /__ /__

_____
_____
_____
_____
_____
_____
_____
_____

"Gratitude dissolves negativity. Decide that no matter what comes your way, you'll find a grateful heart."

- Sandi Krakowski -

Daily Gratitude: Date: __ /__ /__

_____
_____
_____
_____
_____
_____
_____
_____

"The greatest source of happiness is the ability to be grateful at all times."

- Zig Ziglar -

"Enter his gates with thanksgiving and his courts with praise; give thanks to the Lord and praise his name.

-Psalm 100:4

Daily Gratitude: Date: __ / __ / __

_____

_____

_____

_____

_____

_____

_____

_____

_____

"Learn to be thankful for what you already have, while you pursue all that you want."

- Jim Rohn -

Daily Gratitude: Date: __ / __ / __

_____

_____

_____

_____

_____

_____

_____

_____

"Be grateful for who you are and whatever you have. Everything you have is a gift from God."

- Rick Warren -

Daily Gratitude:

_____
_____
_____
_____
_____
_____
_____
_____

"Make it a habit to tell people thank you. To express your appreciation, sincerely and without the expectation of anything in return."

- Ralph Marston -

Daily Gratitude: Date: __ / __ / __

_____
_____
_____
_____
_____
_____
_____
_____

"Gratitude helps us to return to our natural state of joyfulness, where we notice what's right instead of what's wrong."

- M.J. Ryan -

Daily Gratitude:

_____
_____
_____
_____
_____
_____
_____
_____

"Thankfulness redirects our attention from our difficulties to the benefits we enjoy. It's like creating a stockpile of good thoughts for when times are tough."

- Michael Hyatt -

Daily Gratitude:

Date: _ /_ /_

_____
_____
_____
_____
_____
_____
_____
_____

"The Lord lives! Praise be to my Rock! Exalted be my God, the Rock, my Savior!

- 2 Samuel 22:47 -

Daily Gratitude: Date: __ /__ /__

_____
_____
_____
_____
_____
_____
_____
_____
_____
_____

"There is blessing hidden in every trial in life, but you have to be willing to open your heart to see them."

- Anonymous -

Daily Gratitude: Date: __ /__ /__

_____
_____
_____
_____
_____
_____
_____
_____
_____

"Gratitude can change common days into thanksgiving, turn routine jobs into joy, and change ordinary opportunities into blessings."

- William Arthur Ward -

Daily Gratitude: Date: __ / __ / __

_____
_____
_____
_____
_____
_____
_____
_____

"Start bringing gratitude to your experiences, instead of waiting for a positive experience in order to feel grateful."

- Marelisa Fabrega -

Daily Gratitude: Date: __ / __ / __

_____
_____
_____
_____
_____
_____
_____
_____

"If you concentrate on finding whatever is good in every situation, you will discover that your life will suddenly be filled with gratitude, a feeling that nurtures the soul."

- Harold Kushner -

Daily Gratitude: Date: _ /_ /_

_____
_____
_____
_____
_____
_____
_____
_____

"Jesus looked at them and said, 'With man this impossible, but with God all things are possible.'"

- Matthew 19:26 -

Daily Gratitude: Date: _ /_ /_

_____
_____
_____
_____
_____
_____
_____
_____

"I may not have gone where I intended to go, but I think I have ended up where I needed to be."

- Douglas Adams -

Daily Gratitude:

_____

_____

_____

_____

_____

_____

_____

_____

"The only place where your dream becomes impossible is in your own thinking."

- Robert H. Schuller -

Daily Gratitude:

Date: __ / __ / __

_____

_____

_____

_____

_____

_____

_____

_____

"The past has no power over the present moment."

- Eckhart Tolle -

Daily Gratitude: Date: __ /__ /__

_____

_____

_____

_____

_____

_____

_____

_____

"You cannot change reality, but you can control the manner in which you look at things. Your attitude is under your own control. Weed out the negative and focus on the positive!"

- Helen Steiner Rice -

Daily Gratitude: Date: __ /__ /__

_____

_____

_____

_____

_____

_____

_____

_____

"Thanks be to God, who delivers me through Jesus Christ our Lord!"

- Romans 7:25 -

Daily Gratitude: Date: __ / __ / __

_____
_____
_____
_____
_____
_____
_____
_____
_____

"When we give cheerfully and accept gratefully, everyone is blessed."

- Maya Angelou -

Daily Gratitude: Date: __ / __ / __

_____
_____
_____
_____
_____
_____
_____
_____

"As long as this exists, this sunshine and this cloudless sky, and as long as I can enjoy it, how can I be sad?"

- Anne Frank -

"Gratitude lifts our eyes off the things we lack so we might see the blessings we possess.

-Max Lucado

Daily Gratitude:

Date: _ / _ / _

_____
_____
_____
_____
_____
_____
_____
_____
_____

"In ordinary life, we hardly realize that we receive a great deal more than we give, and that it is only with gratitude that life becomes rich."

- Dietrich Bonhoeffer -

Daily Gratitude:

Date: _ / _ / _

_____
_____
_____
_____
_____
_____
_____
_____

"So do not fear, for I am with you; do not be dismayed, for I am your God. I will strengthen you and help you; I will uphold you with my righteous right hand."

- Isaiah 41:10 -

Daily Gratitude:

Date: __ / __ / __

_____
_____
_____
_____
_____
_____
_____
_____
_____

"Gratitude makes sense of our past, brings peace for today, and creates a vision for tomorrow."

- Melody Beattie -

Daily Gratitude:

Date: __ / __ / __

_____
_____
_____
_____
_____
_____
_____
_____

"The most certain sign of wisdom is cheerfulness."

- Michel De Montaigne -

Daily Gratitude: Date: __ /__ /__

_____
_____
_____
_____
_____
_____
_____
_____

"Your attitude not your aptitude will determine your altitude."

- Zig Ziglar -

Daily Gratitude: Date: __ /__ /__

_____
_____
_____
_____
_____
_____
_____
_____

"The best way to show my gratitude to God is to accept
everything, even my problems, with joy."

- Mother Teresa -

Daily Gratitude: Date: __ / __ / __

_____

_____

_____

_____

_____

_____

_____

_____

"May he give you the desire of your heart and make all your plans succeed."

- Psalm 20:40 -

Daily Gratitude: Date: __ / __ / __

_____

_____

_____

_____

_____

_____

_____

_____

"The struggle ends when the gratitude begins."

- Neale Donald Walsch -

Daily Gratitude: Date: __ /__ /__

_____
_____
_____
_____
_____
_____
_____
_____

"Start each day with a positive thought and a grateful heart."

- Roy T. Bennett -

Daily Gratitude: Date: __ /__ /__

_____
_____
_____
_____
_____
_____
_____
_____

"A sense of blessedness comes from a change of heart, not form more blessings."

- Mason Cooley -

Daily Gratitude: Date: __ / __ / __

_____

_____

_____

_____

_____

_____

_____

_____

_____

"So much has been given to me; I have no time to ponder over what which has been denied."

- Helen Keller -

Daily Gratitude: Date: __ / __ / __

_____

_____

_____

_____

_____

_____

_____

_____

"Therefore, since we have been justified through faith, we have peace with god through our Lord Jesus Christ."

- Romans 5:1 -

Daily Gratitude:

_____

_____

_____

_____

_____

_____

_____

_____

"Gratitude is the ability to experience life as a gift. It liberates us from the prison of self-preoccupation."

- John Ortberg -

Daily Gratitude:

Date: __ / __ / __

_____

_____

_____

_____

_____

_____

_____

_____

"There are only two ways to live your life. One is as though nothing is a miracle. The other is as though everything is a miracle."

- Albert Einstein -

Daily Gratitude: Date: __ /__ /__

_____

_____

_____

_____

_____

_____

_____

_____

"Nothing is more honorable than a grateful heart."

- Lucius Annaeus Seneca -

Daily Gratitude: Date: __ /__ /__

_____

_____

_____

_____

_____

_____

_____

_____

"For the wages of sin is death, but the gift of God is eternal life in Christ Jesus our Lord."

- Romans 6:23 -

Daily Gratitude:

_____
_____
_____
_____
_____
_____
_____
_____

"What separates privilege from entitlement is gratitude."

- Brene Brown -

Daily Gratitude:

Date: __ / __ / __

_____
_____
_____
_____
_____
_____
_____
_____

"There are always flowers for those who want to see them."

- Henri Matisse -

"Every good and perfect gift is form above, coming down from the Father of heavenly lights, who does not change like shifting shadows.

-James 1:17

Daily Gratitude: Date: __ /__ /__

_____

_____

_____

_____

_____

_____

_____

_____

"If you don't appreciate what you have, you may as well not have it."

- Rosalene Glickman -

Daily Gratitude: Date: __ /__ /__

_____

_____

_____

_____

_____

_____

_____

_____

"Gratitude changes the pangs of memory into a tranquil joy."

- Dietrich Bonhoeffer -

Daily Gratitude: Date: __ /__ /__

_____

_____

_____

_____

_____

_____

_____

_____

"Gratitude is one of the sweet shortcuts to finding peach of mind and happiness inside. No matter what is going on outside of us, there's always something we could be grateful for."

- Barry Neil Kaufman -

Daily Gratitude: Date: __ /__ /__

_____

_____

_____

_____

_____

_____

_____

"Of the blessings set before you, make your choice, and be content."

- Samuel Johnson -

Daily Gratitude:

_____
_____
_____
_____
_____
_____
_____
_____

"Therefore, since we are receiving a kingdom that cannot be shaken, let us be thankful, and so worship God acceptably with reverence and awe, for our 'God is a consuming fire'."

- Hebrews 12:28-29 -

Daily Gratitude:

Date: __ /__ /__

_____
_____
_____
_____
_____
_____
_____
_____

"What you focus on expands, and when you focus on the goodness in your life, you create more of it."

- Oprah Winfrey -

Daily Gratitude:

_____

_____

_____

_____

_____

_____

_____

_____

_____

"Most human beings have an almost infinite capacity for taking things for granted."

- Aldous Huxley -

Daily Gratitude:

Date: __ /__ /__

_____

_____

_____

_____

_____

_____

_____

_____

"Cultivate the habit of being grateful for every good thing that comes to you, and to give thanks continuously. And because all things have contributed to your advancement, you should include all things in your gratitude."

- Ralph Waldo Emerson -

Daily Gratitude: Date: __ /__ /__

_____
_____
_____
_____
_____
_____
_____
_____
_____

"Gratitude bestows reverence, allowing us to encounter everyday epiphanies, those transcendent moments of awe that change forever how we experience life and the world."

- John Milton -

Daily Gratitude: Date: __ /__ /__

_____
_____
_____
_____
_____
_____
_____
_____

"For everything God created is good, and nothing is to be rejected if it is received with thanksgiving, because it is consecrated by the word of God and prayer."

- 1 Timothy 4:4-5 -

Daily Gratitude: Date: __ /__ /__

_____

_____

_____

_____

_____

_____

_____

_____

"Look at everything as though you were seeing it for the first or the last time, then your time on Earth will be filled with glory."

- Betty Smith -

Daily Gratitude: Date: __ /__ /__

_____

_____

_____

_____

_____

_____

_____

_____

"When we focus on our gratitude, the tide of disappointment goes out and the tide of love rushes in."

- Kristin Armstrong -

Daily Gratitude:

_____
_____
_____
_____
_____
_____
_____
_____
_____

"If you have your health, if you have people in your life to love, you are blessed. Slow down and enjoy the simple things in life."

- Joel Osteen -

Daily Gratitude:

Date: __ / __ / __

_____
_____
_____
_____
_____
_____
_____
_____

"Every breath we draw is a gift of God's love; every moment of existence is a grace."

- Thomas Merton -

Daily Gratitude: Date: __ /__ /__

_____

_____

_____

_____

_____

_____

_____

_____

"O Lord that lends me a life, lend me a heart replete with thankfulness!"

- William Shakspeare -

Daily Gratitude: Date: __ /__ /__

_____

_____

_____

_____

_____

_____

_____

_____

"Let the message of Christ dwell among you richly as you teach and admonish one another with all wisdom through psalms, hymns, songs from the Spirit, singing to God with gratitude in your hearts ."

- Colossians 3:16 -

Daily Gratitude: Date: __ / __ / __

_____
_____
_____
_____
_____
_____
_____
_____

"There are always flowers for those who want to see them."

- Henri Matisse -

Daily Gratitude: Date: __ / __ / __

_____
_____
_____
_____
_____
_____
_____
_____

"Those with a grateful mindset tend to see the message in the mess. And even though life ma knock them down, the grateful find reasons, if even small ones, to get up."

- Steve Maraboli -

"

The direction of the mind is more important than its progress.

-**Joseph Joubert**

Daily Gratitude: Date: __ / __ / __

_____

_____

_____

_____

_____

_____

_____

_____

"The Lord is my strength and my shield; my heart trusts in him, and he helps me. My heart leaps for joy, and with my song I praise him."

- Psalm 28:7 -

Daily Gratitude: Date: __ / __ / __

_____

_____

_____

_____

_____

_____

_____

_____

"The discipline of gratitude is the explicit effort to acknowledge that all I am and have is given to me as a gift of love, a gift to be celebrated with joy."

- Henri Nouwen -

Daily Gratitude: Date: __ /__ /__

_____
_____
_____
_____
_____
_____
_____
_____

"A simple grateful thought turned heavenwards is the most perfect prayer."

- Doris Lessing -

Daily Gratitude: Date: __ /__ /__

_____
_____
_____
_____
_____
_____
_____

"What seems to us as bitter trials are often blessings in disguise."

- Oscar Wilde -

Daily Gratitude: Date: __ /__ /__

_____
_____
_____
_____
_____
_____
_____
_____

"Let us remember that, as much has been given us, much will be expected from us, and that tur homage comes from the heart as well as from the lips, and shows itself in deeds."

- Theodore Roosevelt -

Daily Gratitude: Date: __ /__ /__

_____
_____
_____
_____
_____
_____
_____
_____

"So then, just as you received Christ Jesus as Lord, continue to live your live in him, rooted and built up in him, strengthened in the faith as you were taught, and overflowing with thankfulness."

- Colossians 2:6-7 -

Daily Gratitude: Date: __ /__ /__

_____

_____

_____

_____

_____

_____

_____

_____

"Gratitude for the present moment and the fullness of life now is the true prosperity."

- Eckhart Tolle -

Daily Gratitude: Date: __ /__ /__

_____

_____

_____

_____

_____

_____

_____

_____

"To educate yourself for the feeling of gratitude means to take nothing for granted, but to always seek out and value the kind that will stand behind the action."

- Albert Schweitzer -

Daily Gratitude:

_____
_____
_____
_____
_____
_____
_____
_____

"Our real blessings often appear to us in the shape of pains, losses and disappointments; but let us have patience and we soon shall see them in their proper figures."

- Joseph Addison -

Daily Gratitude: Date: __ / __ / __

_____
_____
_____
_____
_____
_____
_____
_____

"Sing and make music from your heart to the Lord, always giving thanks to God the Father for everything, in the name of our Lord Jesus Christ."

- Ephesians 5:19-20 -

Daily Gratitude: Date: __ /__ /__

_____

_____

_____

_____

_____

_____

_____

_____

_____

"While it may be difficult to change the world, it is always possible to change the way we look at it."

- Matthieu Ricard -

Daily Gratitude: Date: __ /__ /__

_____

_____

_____

_____

_____

_____

_____

_____

"Gratitude is a powerful catalyst for happiness. It's the spark that lights a fire of joy in your soul."

- Amy Collette -

Daily Gratitude: Date: __ /__ /__

_____
_____
_____
_____
_____
_____
_____
_____

"In ordinary life, we hardly realize that we receive a great deal more than we give, and that it is only with gratitude that life becomes rich."

- Dietrich Bonhoeffer -

Daily Gratitude: Date: __ /__ /__

_____
_____
_____
_____
_____
_____
_____
_____

"Joy is the simplest form of gratitude."

- Karl Barth -

Daily Gratitude: Date: __ /__ /__

_____

_____

_____

_____

_____

_____

_____

_____

"Amen! Praise and glory and wisdom and thanks and honor and power and strength be to our god for ever and ever. Amen!"

- Revelation 7:12 -

Daily Gratitude: Date: __ /__ /__

_____

_____

_____

_____

_____

_____

_____

_____

"Gratitude is when memory is stored in the heart and not in the mind."

- Lionel Hampton -

Daily Gratitude:

_____
_____
_____
_____
_____
_____
_____
_____

"Two kinds of gratitude: The sudden kind we feel for what we take; the larger kind we feel for what we give."

- Edwin Arlington Robinson -

Daily Gratitude:

Date: __ / __ / __

_____
_____
_____
_____
_____
_____
_____
_____

"Gratitude is the healthiest of all human emotions. The more you express gratitude for what you have, the more likely you will have even more to express gratitude for."

- Zig Ziglar -

Daily Gratitude:

Date: __ /__ /__

_____
_____
_____
_____
_____
_____
_____
_____
_____

"Don't dig up in doubt what you planted in faith."

- Elisabeth Elliot -

Daily Gratitude:

Date: __ /__ /__

_____
_____
_____
_____
_____
_____
_____
_____

"From them will come songs of thanksgiving and the sound of rejoicing. I will add to their numbers, and they will not be decreased; I will bring them honor, and they will not be disdained."
- Jeremiah 30:19 -

Daily Gratitude: Date: __ / __ / __

_____

_____

_____

_____

_____

_____

_____

_____

"The real gift of gratitude is that the more grateful you are, the more present you become."

- Robert Holden -

Daily Gratitude: Date: __ / __ / __

_____

_____

_____

_____

_____

_____

_____

_____

"In that day you will say: 'Give praise to the Lord, proclaim his name; make known among the nations what he has done, and proclaim that his name is exalted."

- Isaiah 12:4 -

CONNECT WITH DUKE

 @DUKEMATLOCK

 FACEBOOK.COM/DUKEMATLOCK

 INSTAGRAM.COM/DUKEMATLOCK

 LINKEDIN.COM/IN/DUKEMATLOCK1

The best way to guarantee continued growth and ongoing development is to subscribe to my blog. Weekly posts focused on personal and professional development, investing in yourself and success, and leadership will help you cultivate a culture of growth in your life. Subscribe today and stay up to date on everything that is happening at Invest Leadership Initiative.

DUKEMATLOCK.COM

GET UP & GROW AND THE GET UP & GROW JOURNAL AVAILABLE NOW!

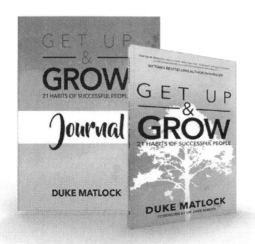

Now available on dukematlock.com, amazon.com, or anywhere books are sold!

MINISTERS MASTERMIND

A community for highly motivated pastors to expand their leadership capacity, share ideas, and build relationships while be challenged and encouraged!

**VISIT
DUKEMATLOCK.COM/MINISTERSMASTERMIND
FOR MORE INFO!**

EXPERIENCE DUKE **LIVE!**

"DUKE'S PRACTICAL APPLICATION OF POWERFUL PRINCIPLES LACED WITH JUST THE RIGHT AMOUNT OF HUMOR CAUSES THE LISTENER TO PURSUE A JOURNEY OF PERSONAL LEADERSHIP GROWTH."

- ED RUSSO
LEAD PASTOR, VICTORIOUS LIFE CHURCH

"DUKE'S COMBINATION OF WISDOM AND HUMOR ENGAGE A FULL AUDITORIUM OR SMALL CONFERENCE ROOM ALIKE. WILLING PARTICIPANTS LEAVE INSPIRED WITH HOPE, AND EQUIPPED WITH THE TOOLS TO MAKE DREAMS COME TRUE."

- MICHAEL H. LINK, MD
FAMILY HEALTH CARE OF CENTRAL FLORIDA

"DUKE'S MINISTY IS ENGAGING AND INSPIRING. HIS COACHING IS FILLED WITH WISDOM AND INSIGHT THAT ACCELEREATES OTHERS! HE HAS A GREAT ABILITY IN HELPING A TEAM BECOME MORE COHESIVE AND FOCUSED ON REACHING THIER GOALS. I CAN HIGHLY RECOMMEND DUKE AS A SPEAKER AND COACH FOR YOU PERSONALLY, AND FOR YOUR TEAM."

- TOM MANNING
LEAD PASTOR, CHRISTIAN LIFE CENTER

FOR MORE ON SHEDULING DUKE TO SPEAK AT YOUR CHURCH, SPECIAL EVENT, OR CONFERENCE

VISIT WWW.DUKEMATLOCK.COM

Made in the USA
Columbia, SC
27 November 2018